Environmental considerations of the NGATS ATM-Airportal Concept

David A. Senzig
Jonathan T. Lee
Volpe National Transportation Systems Center
Cambridge, Massachusetts

January 31, 2008

1 Introduction

This report discusses some of the environmental considerations of the Airportal Concept. This information in this report is based on the NGATS ATM-Airportal Concept by J. Lee, *et al.*, version 1.0 dated September 28, 2007. This report is intended to provide the Airportal project with an overview of environmental aspects of the Airportal Concept document, and to present possible environmental gaps and overlaps with other JPDO projects. This report begins with a general overview of aviation environmental considerations, including a sub-section on how an individual aircraft operation can impact the environment. The next section discusses environmental elements of Airport surface concepts, which is followed by a section on Airportal terminal concepts. The final section discusses some to gaps and overlaps of Airportal relative to some existing programs. A list of acronyms can be found after the main body of the document. Two appendices present details of some of the environmental analyses in the body of the document.

2 Aviation Environmental Considerations

This section discusses general topics in the major environmental areas of noise, emissions, and fuel burn as they related to aviation.

2.1 Noise

The following sub-sections discuss noise effects, metrics, and modeling.

2.1.1 Noise effects

Aviation noise is typically not loud enough to cause hearing loss. The effects of aviation noise are generally considered to consist of short-term physiologic effects, annoyance, speech interference, sleep interference and awakenings, and learning effects. Short-term effects from aircraft noise are similar to other stressors; startle and changes in heart beat patterns are the most common. Annoyance is subjective, with large variability in responses in a given population group; the consensus curve from FICON[1] is shown below in Figure 1. Aircraft (or any other source) noise can drown out or mask speech, making it difficult or impossible to carry on a normal conversation or to hear a desired audio source (e.g. a radio or TV). Noise can also cause sleep interference and awakenings, though some studies show people habituate to noise, leading to a lessened effect. Recent studies have shown correlation between reducing aircraft noise in schools and improved scores on standardized test[2].

---

[1] Federal Interagency Committee On Noise, "Federal agency review of selected airport noise analysis issues, August 1992
[2] Federal Interagency Committee on Aviation Noise, www.fican.org.

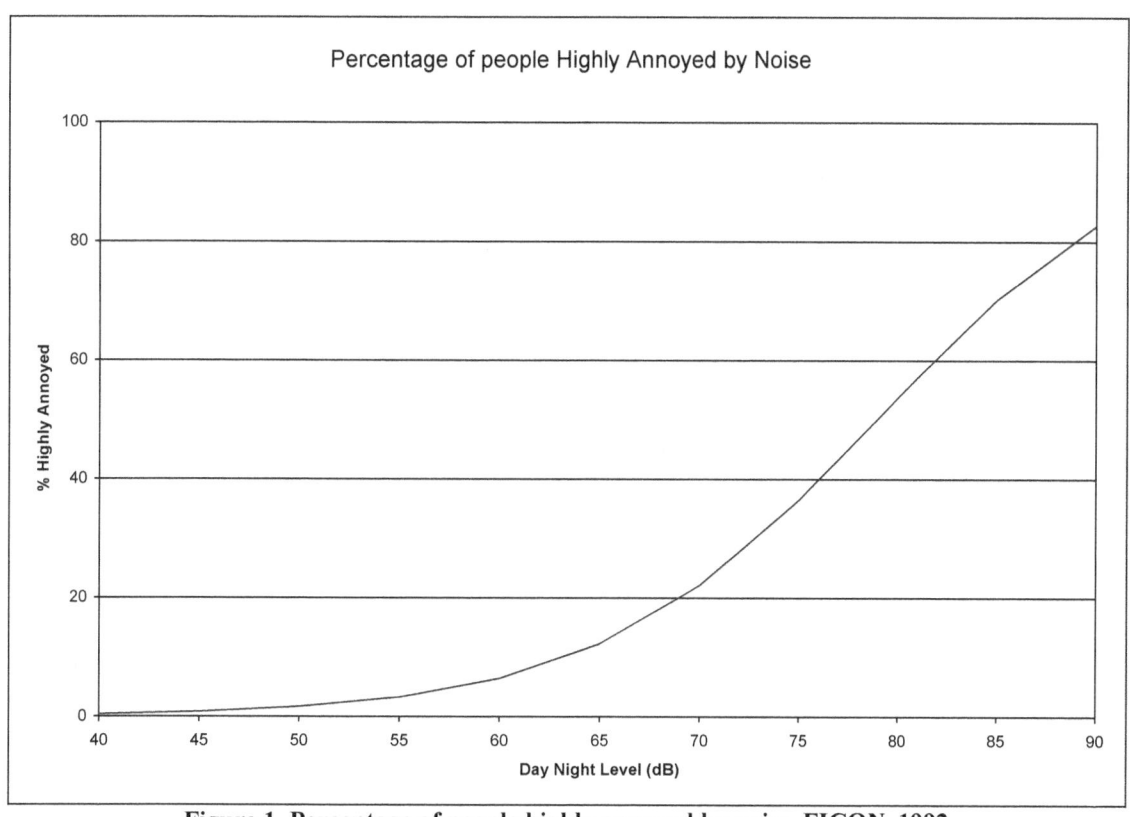

Figure 1, Percentage of people highly annoyed by noise, FICON, 1992

2.1.2 Noise metrics

The primary noise metric used by the FAA is the Day Night Level (DNL). The DNL metric is a 24 hour average A-weighted[3] sound level with a 10 dB penalty added to sound levels in the nighttime period from 10 pm to 7 am[4]. The FAA uses a criterion of 65 dB DNL to determine land use compatibility. The FAA considers residential housing an incompatible land use around an airport when the noise environment is 65 dB DNL or higher. Research has determined that about 12 to 13% of the population is highly annoyed at an exposure level of 65 dB DNL[5]. Many researchers have extensively studied the effects of aircraft noise on sleep.[6] The results of this sleep disturbance research

---

[3] "A-weighting" refers to a frequency weighting that de-emphasizes the low and high frequencies that humans don't hear very well. One can think of A-weighting as a band-pass filter than changes the noise levels so that sound level measuring devices better mimic human hearing.

[4] Harris, Handbook of Acoustical Measurements and Noise Control, 3rd edition, McGraw Hill, 1991

[5] Schultz, J. Acoust. Soc. Am. 64, 377-405 (1978). In 1992, the findings of Schultz were re-confirmed by FICON. However, Schultz and FICON included all transportation sources in the estimation of percent highly annoyed. Current results for aircraft noise only are much closer to 25% highly annoyed at 65 dB DNL. (Miedema, H.M.E, and C.G.M. Oudshoorn, "Annoyance from Transportation Noise: Relationships with Exposure Metrics DNL and DENL and Their Confidence Intervals" Environmental Health Perspectives, Vol. 109 No. 4, 2001, pp. 409-416) (Fidell, S. and L. Silvati "Parsimonious alternatives to regression analysis for characterizing prevalence rates of aircraft noise annoyance," Noise Control Eng. J. 53(2), 2004 Mar-Apr)

[6] Ollerhead, J.B., et al, "Report of a Field Study of Aircraft Noise and Sleep Disturbance," Department of Transport, December 1992

Fidell, S., et al, "Noise-Induced Sleep Disturbance in Residential Settings," AL/OE-TR-1994-0131, February 1994

suggest that cumulative metrics (such as DNL) do not correlate well with sleep disturbance. Hence the effects of aircraft operations occurring later in the evening or earlier in the morning may not be accurately represented by changes in DNL.

In addition to absolute levels of noise, the FAA also considers that changes in noise exposure can be significant based on prior (pre-existing) noise levels. These noise change criteria are meant to protect areas farther from the airport than would be solely based on the 65 DNL criteria. Table 1 below shows the FAA's criteria[7] for significant noise level changes. An example of significant noise impact would be an area that currently has a noise exposure level of 50 dB DNL from aircraft activity at multiple airports. This area, after an airspace change, is predicted to have a noise exposure level of 58 dB DNL. The FAA considers this a significant change because even though this level is below the 65 dB DNL criteria, it is a change of more than 5 dB in a multiple airport study with a base noise level between 45 and 60 dB.

Table 1, Noise Impact Criteria

Study Type	Noise Level (DNL)			
	< 45 dB	45 – 60 dB	60 – 65 dB	> 65 dB
Single airport	-	-	±3 dB	±1.5 dB
Multiple airports	-	±5 dB	±3 dB	±1.5 dB

2.1.3 Noise modeling

Analysts currently model aviation noise with the FAA's Integrated Noise Model (INM) when a single airport is under consideration or with the FAA's Noise Integrated Routing System (NIRS) when a wide area or multiple airports are to be considered. The FAA is in the process of replacing their existing noise and emissions models with a single Aviation Environmental Design Tool (AEDT)[8]. AEDT, with its common operations data, will allow easier determination of relationships between noise, emission, and fuel consumption.

2.2 Emissions

The following sub-sections discuss emission effects, metrics, and modeling.

Fidell, S., et al, "Noise-Induced Sleep Disturbance Near Two Civil Airports," NASA Report 198252, Dec. 1995

Basner, M., et al, "Effects of Nocturnal Aircraft Noise, Volume 1, Executive Summary," German Aerospace Center (DLR), Institute of Aerospace Medicine, Flightphysiology Department, Linder Hoehe, 51147 Cologne, Germany, July 2004

Passchier-Vermeer, et al, "Sleep disturbance and aircraft noise exposure, Exposure-effect relationships," TNO Report number 2002.027, June 2002

[7] The criteria are from FAA Order 1050.1E, June 8, 2004.

[8] The AEDT will incorporate all INM functions; the functionality of NIRS will be retained, but the interface between AEDT and NIRS is currently under review by the FAA's AEE and ATO organizations.

2.2.1 Emissions effects

Analysts currently track the following aircraft emissions: Carbon Dioxide (CO_2), Carbon Monoxide (CO), unburned Hydrocarbons (HC)[9], Hazardous Air Pollutants (HAP), Nitrogen Oxides (NO_x), Sulfur Oxides (SO_x), and Particulate Matter (PM). We can generally classify the emissions as green house gases (CO_2), or local air quality pollutants (the others), except for NOx, which is both a greenhouse gas and a local air quality pollutant. The green house effects of aircraft condensation trails (contrails) are not currently modeled[10].

The effects of aircraft emissions on the current and projected climate of our planet may be the most serious long-term environmental issue facing the aviation industry. The climatic impacts of aviation emissions include the direct climate effects from CO2 and water vapor emissions, the indirect forcing on climate resulting from changes in the distributions and concentrations of ozone and methane as a consequence of aircraft NOx emissions, the direct effects (and indirect effects on clouds) from emitted aerosols and aerosol precursors, and the climate effects associated with contrails and cirrus cloud formation[11].

The EPA tracks levels of CO, NOx, SOx and PM in the air; these, in addition to lead and ozone, are considered by the EPA to be the six principle air pollutants[12]. The health effects of CO at low concentrations are fatigue in healthy people and chest pain in people with heart disease, and at higher concentrations include impaired vision and coordination, headaches, dizziness, confusion, and nausea. NOx emissions are a precursor to ozone. Ozone is by far the principle air quality problem in U.S. cities today. According to EPA data, as of 2005, there were 474 counties out of 3,142 nationally that do not meet the EPA's 8-hour ozone standard and are considered non-attainment areas[13]. Peak levels of SO_2 in the air can cause temporary breathing difficulty for people with asthma who are active outdoors. Longer-term exposures to high levels of SO_2 gas and particles cause respiratory illness and aggravate existing heart disease. Particular Matter is divided into fine (less than 2.5 micrometers) or course (2.5 to 10 micrometers). PM is a health hazard due to the ability of the particles to enter the lungs. Long-term exposures of a year or more have been linked to the development of lung diseases, such as chronic bronchitis[14].

2.2.2 Emissions metrics

The emission input parameters are given as a total mass of each emission produced per unit of engine thrust. These parameters are referred to as Emission Indices (EI). The EI for a particular aircraft is a function of aircraft power state. ICAO provides EI for four

---

[9] Another term sometimes used for HC emissions is Volatile Organic Compounds (VOC) emissions

[10] The contrail effects on climate change are not well understood. Contrails may be net thermal reflectors during the day, but may act as thermal blankets (by inhibiting thermal radiation from the earth's surface) at night. Stanford University, funded by FAA's PARTNER program has recently launched a study of this effect.

[11] "A Report of Findings and Recommendations," Workshop on the Impacts of Aviation on Climate Change, June 7-9, 2006, Boston.

[12] http://www.epa.gov/air/urbanair/index html

[13] "Aviation & Emissions, a Primer", FAA Office of Environment and Energy, January 2005.

[14] http://airnow.gov/index.cfm?action=static.aqguidepart

power states: 100% - used for takeoff power, 85% - used for climb-out power, 30% - used for arrival power, 7% - used for idle and taxi power. Note that the four ICAO power states are intended for use in the terminal area to assist with local air quality analyses, they are not intended to capture en-route cruise conditions. The output metrics are an inventory of the masses of the pollutants generated, either on a short-term (hourly) or long-term (yearly) scale. Figure 2, Figure 3, and Figure 4 below show the EI for three pollutants for an engine in use on the Boeing 737-700[15]. The figures show that NO_x is directly related to thrust, while CO and HC are inversely related to thrust. NO_x is produced when Nitrogen (N_2) in air disassociates in the combustion process due high temperatures and then bonds with available Oxygen. NO_x production is a function of the amount of air exposed to the combustion process, and therefore tracks the thrust setting. CO and HC are by-products of incomplete combustion, which tends to occur at low power settings when the internal temperatures and pressures are lower.

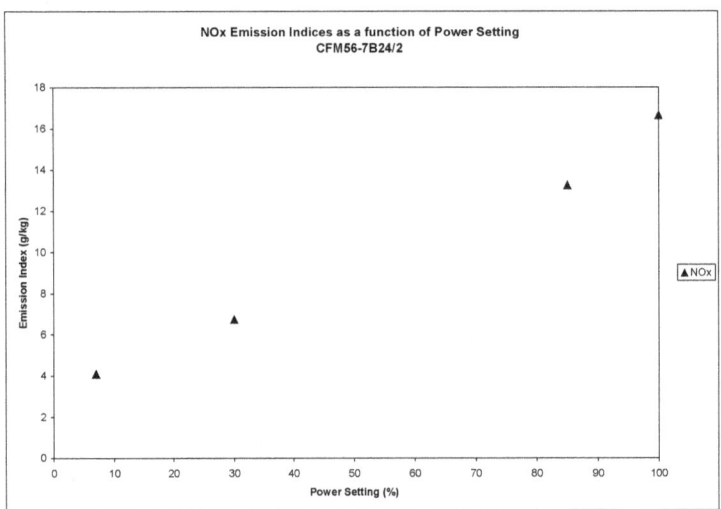

Figure 2, Nitrogen Oxides Emissions Indices example

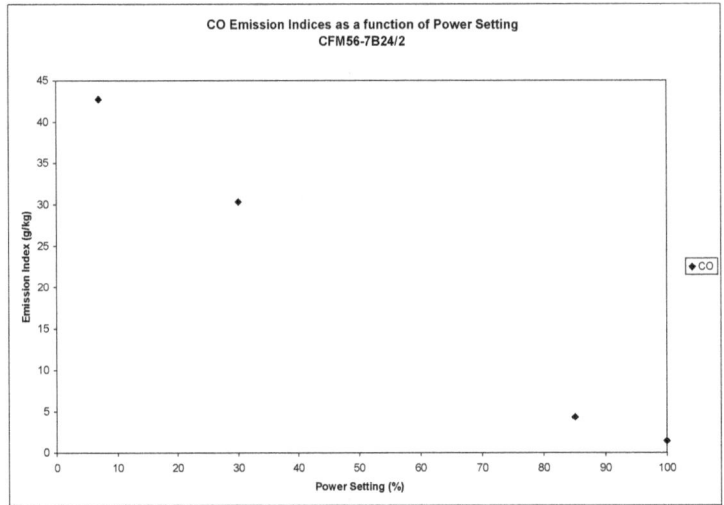

Figure 3, Carbon Monoxide Emissions Indices example

---

[15] EI interpolation is not linear, so lines connecting the points are not shown.

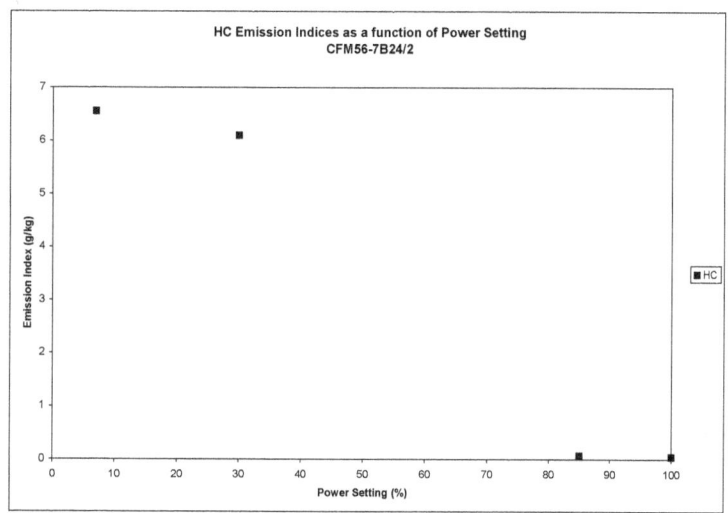

Figure 4, Unburned Hydrocarbons Emission Indices Example

ICAO has been increasing the stringency of NOx emissions for the last several years. Increased stringency means less NOx can be produced for each unit of thrust from the engine; the units used in the ICAO requirements are grams of NOx per kilonewton (kN) of thrust. The NOx requirements for large turbofan engines (over 20,000 lb static thrust) are given in term of the Overall Pressure Ratio (OPR). The OPR is the ratio of the maximum compression of the air within the engine[16] to the air pressure at ambient conditions.

Table 2, Changes in NOX stringency

Year	ICAO meeting	OPR limits	Emission Equation	Reduction
1981	CAEE	-	40 + 2*OPR	-
1993	CAEP/2	-	32+1.6*OPR	20% from CAEE
1999	CAEP/4	Below 30	19 + 1.6*OPR	16% from CAEP/2
		Above 30	7 + 2*OPR	
2004	CAEP/6	Below 30	16.72 + 1.408*OPR	12% from CAEP/4
		Above 30	-1.04 + 2*OPR	

The NO_x stringency requirements listed in Table 2 above are also presented in graphical form in Figure 5 below.

---

[16] This maximum pressure occurs after the last stage of the engine's compressor, just before the air enters the combustor.

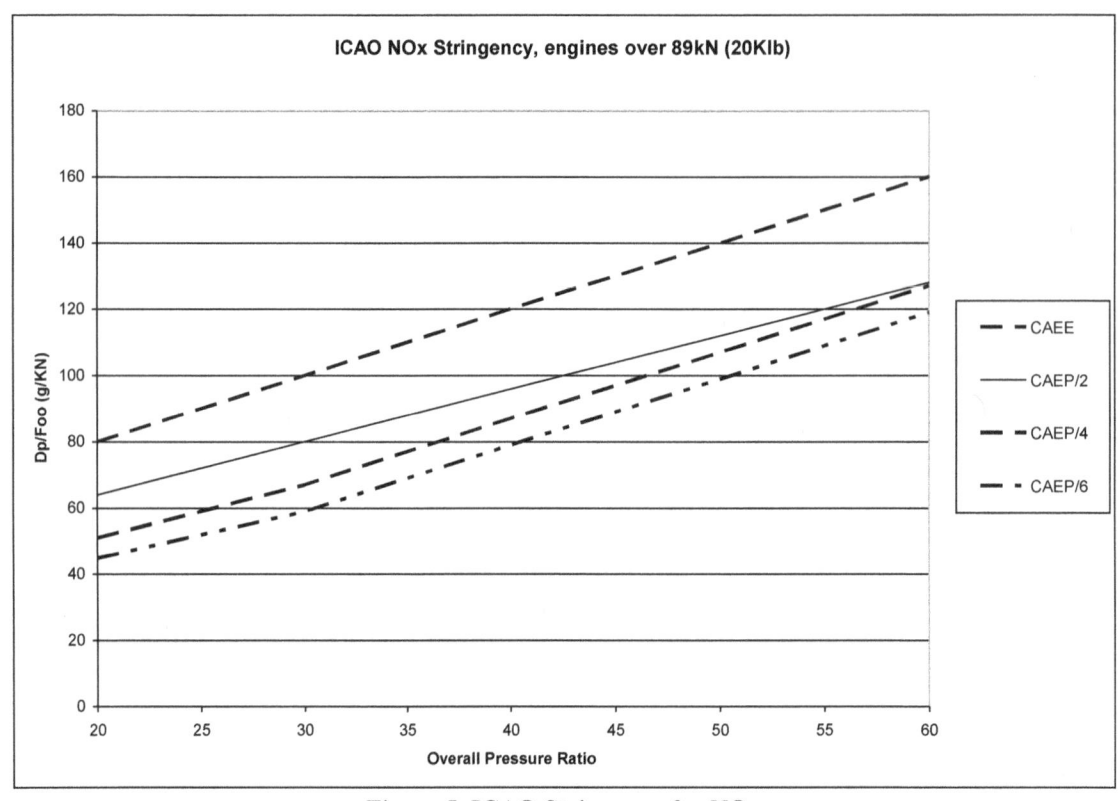

Figure 5, ICAO Stringency for NOx

2.2.3 Emissions modeling

Analysts currently use the FAA's Emissions & Dispersion Modeling System (EDMS) to model local air quality impacts. EDMS models NO_x, CO, SO_x, and PM emissions for operations both on the ground and in the air. Operations in the air are typically modeled up to 3000 feet AFE, which is generally taken as the top of the atmospheric mixing layer[17]. As mentioned in Section 2.1 above, the FAA is currently in the process of replacing EDMS with AEDT.

2.3 Fuel Consumption

The following sub-sections discuss fuel consumption effects, metrics and modeling.

2.3.1 Fuel consumption effects

Major effects of fuel consumption are reductions in total fossil fuel energy available, global climate change, and economic impacts. None of these effects are local problems specific to a particular airport.

A GAO report has stated that oil production will likely peak sometime in the next 35 years[18]. Though small in terms of percentage of total use (currently around 2%), aviation

---

[17] Aircraft emissions produced below the atmospheric mixing layer are assumed to remain in the local environment, while those produced above this layer are assumed to not contribute to the local environment. The height of the mixing layer is determined by local temperature profiles and turbulence conditions.

[18] "Crude Oil: Uncertainty about future oil supply makes it important to develop a strategy for addressing a peak and decline in oil production," GAO report GAO-07-283, February 2007

fuel use is expected to become an increasing percentage of total oil consumed as aviation grows relative to other transportation modes. Reducing aviation fuel consumption will lower general fuel consumption, extending the fossil fuel supply until alternatives can be developed.

Fuel costs are currently the airlines largest direct operating costs. Reducing fuel consumption will directly improve the airlines' financial health. The Air Transport Association reports[19] that in the 3rd quarter of 2007, fuel was 26.5% of total airline costs, with labor, the next highest category, at 23.4% of total costs.

2.3.2 Fuel consumption metrics

Fuel consumption is tracked by volume of jet fuel (JP-1A and JP-1) used by the turbine-powered fleet. Aviation gasoline ("Avgas") used in piston engine aircraft is not currently tracked due to the small amount consumed compared with the turbine fleet and the less reliable operations data associated with the piston engine General Aviation fleet.

2.3.3 Fuel consumption modeling

Fuel consumption is currently modeled with the FAA's System for assessing Aviation's Global Emissions (SAGE). As with the INM and EDMS models, SAGE will also be incorporated into AEDT. Note that for those parts of flight above 10,000 feet, SAGE calculates fuel burn (and the associated emissions) using the coefficients and equations of EUROCONTROL's Base of Aircraft Data (BADA). Table 3 below summarizes the models currently used for aviation environmental analyses.

Table 3, Summary of Aviation Environmental Models

Environmental Issue	Current Model	Current Version (release year)	Future Model
Noise	Integrated Noise Model (INM)	7.0 (2007)	Aviation Environmental Design Tool (AEDT) – public release of version 2.0 expected in 2011
Air Quality	Emission and Dispersion Modeling System (EDMS)	5.0.2 (2007)	
Fuel Consumption	System for assessing Aviation's Global Emissions (SAGE)	1.5 (2005)	

2.4 Single Operations Analysis

This sub-section examines the environmental effects of a typical flight from the departure gate to the arrival gate, broken out by operational regime.

---

[19] http://www.airlines.org/economics/finance/Cost+Index htm

2.4.1 Departure gate

The noise in this region is due to engines idling and the operation of the Auxiliary Power Unit (APU – a small gas turbine engine typically located in the tail of modern aircraft). Usually, noise in this region has been considered an occupational hazard issue for the workers near the aircraft, not a community noise issue except for communities abutting the airport property. Emissions are primarily due to engines idling and the APU, with CO and HC as the pollutants of concern. Ground Support Equipment (GSE) can also contribute to the emissions in this region.

2.4.2 Taxi from gate to runway

The noise in this region is due to engines at relatively low power, but with occasional increases during break-away (the increased thrust required to get the aircraft moving after coming to a stop, e.g. while waiting in a take-off queue). The emissions are those generated during low power operations, primarily CO and HC. Fuel burn is relatively low in these operations, about a half a pound a second per engine for a 777, but because these operations may be on the order of tens of minutes, the absolute fuel burn can be as great as that used in the initial departure.

2.4.3 Departure

The noise here is due to engines operating at the high power required for take-off. The noise may be an issue for communities beyond the localized airport area. The emissions are those associated with high power operations, primarily NO_x, CO_2, and PM. This is the region of maximum fuel flow; on a 777, the fuel flow can be as high as 10 pound per second per engine. From the start of the takeoff roll to the cut-back to the maximum climb power altitude of 1,500 AFE takes about 80 seconds for a 777; the exact times will depend on the actual engine power and aircraft weights of the particular takeoff.

2.4.4 Climb out

The aircraft is still generating significant noise due to the engines operating at high power; the noise may be an issue for communities beyond the localized airport area. The emissions are also those associated with high power, primarily NO_x, and CO_2; the NO_x production will have dropped off significantly from the levels generated at departure. The fuel flow drops commensurately with the power reduction; in our 777 example, the fuel flow drops to around 7 to 8 pounds per second per engine at the mixing layer.

2.4.5 Cruise

En-route noise is not generally a concern. Emissions of concern are CO_2, NO_x, PM, and H_2O, with H_2O of concern because of contrail formation and the addition of water vapor into the stratosphere. Aircraft with turbofan engines are most efficient at high altitudes; the 777 in our example is now burning about 2 pounds per second per engine.

2.4.6 Descent

Noise is generally not a concern in this region. The emissions in this region are those associated with low power, primarily CO and VOC. Fuel burn is low, but dependent on the speed and angle of descent.

2.4.7 Approach

The noise in this region is due to engines at low power and aerodynamic airframe noise. The aerodynamic airframe noise is primarily due to the high lift devices (e.g. flaps and slats) and the landing gear. While the absolute noise level during approach is less than during departure, the altitude above the ground is less, so approach noise can be as significant a problem as departure noise in the localized area near the airport. Reverse thrust and braking noise can also be a factor while the aircraft is slowing down on the runway after landing. The emissions are those due to low power, primarily CO and HC. The fuel burn is also low, and depends upon the winds and details of the approach; when the landing gear and the high-lift devices are deployed, the fuel burn can rise significantly from the clean configuration used in the initial descent.

2.4.8 Taxi from runway to gate

The taxi issues for returning to a gate are same as when departing from one.

2.4.9 Arrival gate

The issues at the arrival gate are the same those at the departure gate.

The environmental aspects of a single aviation operation are summarized in Table 4 below.

Table 4, Summary of environmental aspects in different flight regimes

Environmental issue	Ground ops	Departure	Climb-out	Cruise	Descent (flaps and gear retracted)	Approach (flaps and gear extended)
Noise impact area	local	regional	regional	-	-	local
Primary emission concern	CO, HC	NO_x	NO_x	CO_2, H_2O	CO, HC	CO, HC
Example 777 fuel flow (lb/sec/engine)	0.5	10	7	2	0.5	2

3 Surface Concept Elements

All elements of surface concepts in the Airportal Concepts document affect fuel usage, noise, and emissions, but the effect varies depending on the particular concept as discussed below. In the discussions below, the individual concepts are compared to the baseline case of operations in today's environment.

3.1 Runway Management

Runway management addresses which runways are used for arrivals and departures and which aircraft will use a particular runway. Runway usage will directly affect the noise exposure for those residences located near the active arrival and departure runways; the actual noise impact at a particular airport would be highly dependent on the runway lay-out and the local population distribution.

Fuel consumption and emissions will be affected by the transition between the terminal and en-route operations (where the aircraft enters/leaves terminal area and the corresponding altitude) and by changes in track distance due to changes in routing. As with noise, the in-flight impacts of the runway management would be highly dependent on the actual runway layout and the departure/arrival operations. Utilizing runways closer to the gate area will tend to reduce fuel consumption and those emissions (CO and HC) with high EI during the relatively low temperature/power settings used in ground operations.

3.2 Taxi Route Planning

Taxi route planning primarily affects fuel burn and a sub-set of emissions. Noise typically is not an issue during taxi operation, though some airports in highly urbanized areas (e.g. Midway in Chicago) do need to consider noise from taxi operations. The primary emissions of interest are CO and HC. These are the emissions which have elevated EI when aircraft turbine engines are operating at the relatively low temperature/power settings used in ground operations. Fuel burn would also be reduced due to more efficient ground movements.

3.3 Super Density Operations

Super Density Operations (SDO) impact will increase the noise, emissions, and fuel burn in a given airport. We expect the noise, emissions and fuel burn to increase proportionally to the increase in the numbers of operations; this proportional increase would apply to all categories of pollutants. The environmental impact per operation would not be significantly different from current operations.

As an example of the impact of SDO, Table 5 below shows the change in noise impacts due to changes in operations at JFK. The baseline data for operations at JFK are taken from an ICAO study undertaken in support of analyzing global noise impacts. Operations increases are taken from JPDO expectations of 2X and 3X current operations. Fleet changes are based on the JPDO's EWG estimates for next generation aircraft in the 150- and 300-seat class; the existing fleet uses current technology aircraft, the new technology fleet replaces the 150 and 300-seat class aircraft, while leaving the other aircraft unchanged.

An alternative method of considering increased operations is to examine the effect of fleet mix to larger aircraft. In this case, we consider the effect of doubling and tripling the

12

numbers of operations as discussed above, but then scale the aircraft operations by moving the associated numbers of passengers from a smaller seat class aircraft to a larger one. This fleet shift has the effect of doubling or tripling the numbers of passengers, but with fewer than a doubling or tripling of aircraft operations. The results of the analysis with these fleet changes are shown in Table 5 below.

Table 5, Noise impacts of SDO operations at JFK, 65 DNL Area in sq. miles

Fleet	1X (baseline) operations	2X (200%) operations	3X (300%) operations
Existing	5.0	9.2	12.6
New technology	-	6.0	8.6
New technology with Fleet Shift	-	5.3	7.8

The details of these analyses are presented in Appendix A. The noise analyses were conducted with the FAA's Integrated Noise Model, version 7.0.

3.4 Surface Weather

Weather can impact runway usage, as well as routing in the terminal area. In general, these changes air traffic management cannot be known a priori, and so are difficult to predict. Given the small numbers of operations affected, this should be considered a lower priority for environmental consideration.

3.5 Summary

The following table summarizes the effects of the Surface Concept Elements on the three metrics of interest. The table represents the impact per operation, not the total impact if the particular Concept allowed operations to increase.

Table 6, General environmental impacts of Surface Concept Elements per operation

Concept	Noise	Emissions	Fuel burn
Runway Management	Not significant	Reduced	Reduced
Taxi Route Planning	Not significant	Reduced	Reduced
Super Density Operations	Not significant	Not significant	Not significant
Surface Weather	Not significant	Not significant	Not significant

4 Terminal Concept Elements

4.1 Precise Spacing and Separation Assurance

Reducing the time and distance between aircraft will cause noise levels to rise due the increase in operations, though individual operations will not change. The increased numbers of operations will also cause a proportionate increase in local emissions and fuel burn. We would expect a general increase in all categories of pollutants.

4.2 Dynamic Airspace Management

Dynamic Airspace Management is unlikely to cause a significant noise impact except that due to the possible overall increase in operations. If Dynamic Airspace Management reduces delays and holds (both on the ground and in the air), fuel burn can be decreased and local air quality improved. Because airborne holds and delays always occur above the mixing layer, the primary reduction in local pollutants would be in HC and CO, which are associated with low power ground operations.

4.3 Adapting Operations to Conditions

Noise, as discussed above, is calculated based on average daily conditions. Non-normal operations would have little impact on DNL numbers as required by the FAA, but could have a large impact on the actual noise environment during periods of non-normal operations[20]. Similarly, emission sand fuel burn would also be affected, but only temporarily and so are difficult to predict.

4.4 Metroplex Operations

We can consider Metroplex operations to be of two types; the first where operations at an existing airport would migrate to a currently underutilized airport, and the second where operations at a number of airports in a region are more closely coordinated.

4.4.1 Metroplex Operations – underutilized airports

Local noise environments within the metroplex region would change significantly under this concept. The FAA's criteria of considering a change of 5 dB as significant (see Table 1 above in section 2.1.2) when the existing aviation noise environment is between 45 and 60 would likely be a significant component of a metroplex study where operations move to an underutilized airport. An earlier EPA report[21] determined that an activity (such as aircraft operations) which increased the noise in a location by 5 dB DNL would lead to widespread complaints. To put this in perspective, a single 737-700 departure is enough to generate a DNL of 50 dB about a mile and a half from the start of the takeoff roll. If this single daily operation were to occur at an airport with no previous jet traffic, both the FAA's and the EPA's significant impact criterion could be met. *Bringing in multiple jet arrival and departure operations, where none existed prior, would almost certainly invite legal action against the airport proprietor.* We will need to choose the metroplex reliever airports with care and either prepare the community for the expected change in noise exposure or prepare ourselves for the expected community reaction.

While emissions would likely increase at the airport which receive more traffic, those emissions would be balanced by the corresponding reduction at airport which is off-

---

[20] The FAA's required noise impact metric is annual average DNL, but supplemental metrics, such as an individual day's DNL, can be produced.

[21] "Information on levels of environmental noise requisite to protect public health and welfare with an adequate margin of safety," EPA 550/9-74-004, March 1974 page D-20. "The data ... indicate that widespread complaints may be expected when the normalized value of the outdoor day-night sound level of the intruding noise exceeds that existing without the intruding noise by approximately 5 dB, and vigorous community reaction may be expected when the excess approaches 20 dB."

loading traffic. An aircraft is as likely to have its travel distance increased as reduced, so we expect no general change in emissions or fuel over the entire metroplex region.

4.4.2 Metroplex Operations – coordinated region

In this case, we assume that the existing airports continue to receive the same operations the have in the past, but the coordination of arrival, departure, and over-flight operations would be conducted to minimize the adverse impacts of regional congestion on individual flights.

As an example of the impact of Metroplex operations in a region serviced by existing airports, Table 7 below shows the change in noise impacts due to changes in operations in the New York Metroplex area. The baseline data for operations at Kennedy, LaGuardia, and Newark airports are taken from an ICAO study undertaken in support of analyzing global noise impacts. Operations increases are taken from JPDO expectations of 2X and 3X current operations. Fleet changes are based on the JPDO's EWG estimates for next generation aircraft in the 150- and 300-seat class. 'Hold-down' operations are those involving an altitude restriction on departing aircraft – these are representative of current operations; 'unrestricted' operations assume no restrictions in aircraft operations – i.e., the Airportal Metroplex concept allows traffic resolutions that don't impact normal departure procedures. The details of this noise analysis are presented in Appendix B.

Note that in results shown in Table 7 below, the noise metric used is the 45 DNL contour. This metric is a reasonable one to use to capture the noise differences due to overlapping operations from different airports. The 65 DNL contours will typically only capture the noise impact from one airport, but the 45 DNL contour represents lower noise level subject to influence by more than a single airport. We anticipate that any fleet mix changes as discussed in section 3.3 above would have similar impacts on noise, emissions, and fuel burn as presented in that section – the impacts of new fleet mixes and new airframe/engine technology are independent of the operational issues discussed here.

Table 7, Noise impacts of Metroplex operations in the NYC Metroplex, 45 DNL Area in sq. miles

Departure Procedure	Fleet	1X (baseline) operations	2X (200%) operations	3X (300%) operations
Hold-down	Existing	436.1	601.2	695.5
	New technology	-	465.1	574.0
Un-restricted	Existing	401.2	538.2	621.5
	New technology	-	431.8	527.6

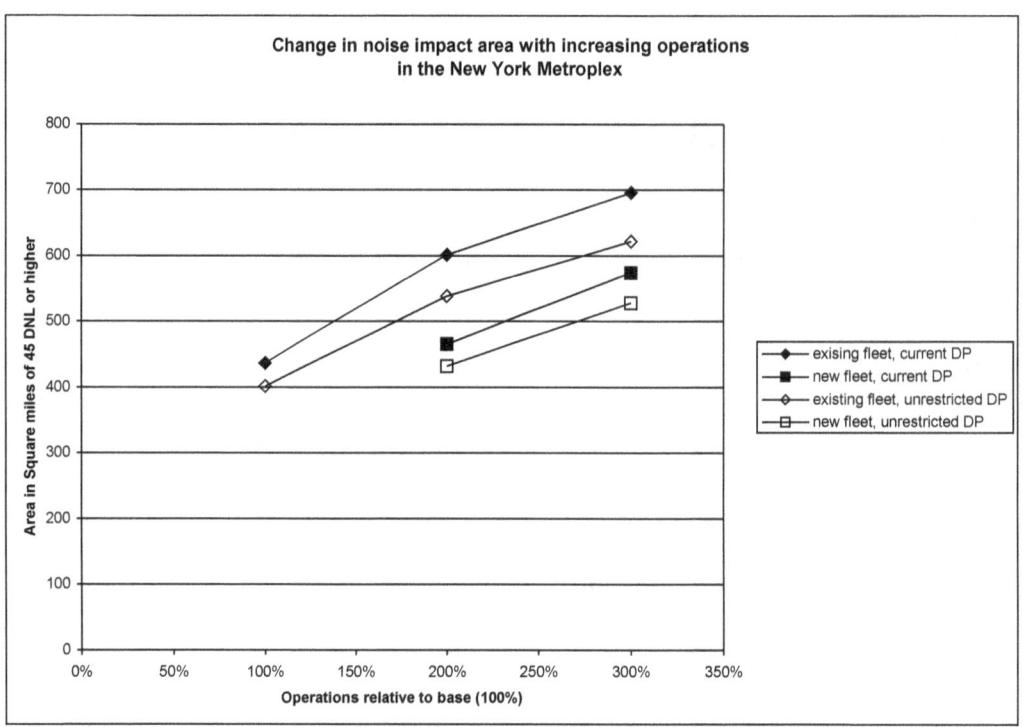

Figure 6, Graphic of data in Table 4

If, in the unrestricted case, traffic conflicts between aircraft operating at different airports could be coordinated such that direct routing could be used, a fuel burn benefit would result. For example, aircraft operating between JFK and Oakland, California (OAK) would have the fuel burn reduction shown in Table 8 below if direct routing out of JFK could be used instead the current routing to the south to avoid conflicts with ERW.

Table 8, Fuel burn per flight, JFK to OAK

Aircraft (seat class)	Current routing	Direct routing	Savings per flight
150	14,347 kg	14,221 kg	127 kg
210	17,493 kg	17,338 kg	155 kg
300	33,479 kg	33,183 kg	297 kg

4.5 Summary

Table 9 below summarizes the effects of the Terminal Concept Elements on the three environmental areas of interest. The table represents the impact per operation, not the total impact if the particular Concept allows operations to increase.

Table 9, General environmental impacts of Terminal Concept Elements per operation

Concept	Noise	Emissions	Fuel burn
Precise Spacing	Not significant	Not significant	Not significant
Dynamic Airspace Management	Not significant	Reduced	Reduced
Adapting Operations	Not significant	Not significant	Not significant
Metroplex – underutilized airports	Locally increased	Not significant	Not significant
Metroplex – coordinated region	Not significant	Reduced	Reduced

5 Potential Gaps and Overlaps

This section discusses possible environmental gaps and overlaps between other federal organizations (such as JPDO and FAA) and the Airportal surface and terminal concept elements. The environmental gaps can be considered research gaps – until the research establishes methods for analysis of the particular issue, practical models can't be implemented.

5.1 Surface Concept Elements

This section discusses potential environmental gaps and overlaps between other federal organizations and the Airportal surface concept elements.

5.1.1 Potential Noise gaps

The FAA's environmental prediction tools currently can predict aircraft noise during runway operations. The algorithms for predicting the noise behind the aircraft during the start of the departure take-off ground roll are currently being upgraded. In addition, the noise during the landing roll, primarily thrust-reverser noise, is under examination by the FAA's Partnership for Air Transportation Noise and Emission Reduction (PARTNER) team for possible improvement in the prediction models. The FAA has considered taxi noise as a possible research topic, but as of this writing, no taxi or gate-operation noise is included in the prediction models.

5.1.2 Potential Emission and fuel burn gaps

The FAA's environmental prediction tools currently calculate emission and fuel burn during ground operations by using times-in-mode calculations. This process requires the user to know the taxi times for particular aircraft. The tools do not currently capture the effects of starting, stopping, idling, and adding 'break-away' power on the journey between the gate and the runway.

5.1.3 Potential Overlaps

The environmental team within JPDO's SMAD has identified sensitivity studies of the impacts of new runways and improved surface and traffic modeling as potential areas of work. These are not intended as full NAS-wide analyses nor as explicit environmental sensitivity studies, but should be coordinated with SMAD to ensure no overlap occurs.

5.2 Terminal Concept Elements

This section discusses the known environmental gaps and overlaps between other federal organizations and Airportal terminal concept elements.

5.2.1 Potential Noise gaps

Most major airports in the U.S. have noise monitoring systems which continuously collect noise and operations data from aircraft terminal operations. These monitoring systems represent an under-utilized resource: the data is used only locally and only in a 'post-mortem' way. These data could be used to develop a national database to assess the efficacy of noise reduction operations. They could also be used as a database for short-term empirical predictions of noise, such as when meteorological effects like temperature inversions lower the accuracy of the standard prediction tools; this would be of use to ATC personnel during runway management decisions.

5.2.2 Potential Emission and fuel burn gaps

The Airportal and Airspace projects currently have no known environmental terminal element gaps with emission and fuel burn[22].

5.2.3 Potential Overlaps

The JPDO Environmental Working Group (EWG) currently has an Operations Standing Committee[23] which is investigating the impacts of Continuous Descent Approaches (CDA) and Metroplex operations on the NAS. Existing work with CDA and Metroplex operations should be coordinated with Airportal work on all aspects of terminal operations.

The FAA has recently announced the Aviation Interoperability Initiative to Reduce Emissions (AIRE). This program will be performing case studies on CDA/Tailored Approaches and surface movement support tools to determine if they can be expanded from the test airports to the NAS. While not an explicit overlap, the Airportal team should maintain an awareness of this program.

The JPDO SMAD has conducted inventories of noise impacts at the 35 OEP airports as well as fuel burn and emissions for operations to and from the top 100 U.S. airports. These inventories have modeled operations within the terminal area down to the surface. SMAD intends to continue these inventories as more data on future fleets and operations become available. The environmental team within SMAD has identified expansion of the noise inventory to include the top 100 airports as a potential area of work in FY2008. The Airspace and Airportal teams should ensure that any individual airport analyses are coordinated, particularly regarding future fleets, operations, and airport layouts.

5.3 Conclusions

We believe the existing analysis tools are adequate to determine the impacts of proposed Airportal actions in the air. The primary gap in potential Airportal environmental analyses are in taxi and ground operations; noise is currently not analyzed for ground operations, the models for air quality and fuel burn may not adequately capture the effects of ground delays. Research into methods to analyze ground operation noise, fuel burn, and emission may be needed to close this gap in our analyses.

---

[22] There are known prediction issues in the terminal area, but these are practical modeling issus, not a research gap or overlap issues.
[23] Led by Everett Palmer of NASA-Ames.

6 Acronyms

AEDT .... Aviation Environmental Design Tool
AFE .... Above Field Elevation
AIRE .... Atlantic Interoperability Initiative to Reduce Emissions
APU .... Auxiliary Power Unit
BADA .... Base of Aircraft Data
CAEP .... Committee on Aviation Environmental Protection
CDA .... Continuous Descent Approach
CO .... Carbon Monoxide
CO_2 .... Carbon Dioxide
Db .... decibels
DNL .... Day-Night Level
DP .... Departure Procedure
EDMS .... Emission & Dispersion Modeling System
EI .... Emission Index (or Indices)
EPA .... Environmental Protection Agency
EWG .... Environmental Working Group
FAA .... Federal Aviation Administration
FICAN .... Federal Interagency Committee on Aviation Noise
FICON .... Federal Interagency Committee on Noise
GAO .... Government Accounting Office
GSE .... Ground Support Equipment
HAP .... Hazardous Air Pollutant
HC .... Hydrocarbon
ICAO .... International Civil Aviation Organization
INM .... Integrated Noise Model
JPDO .... Joint Program Development Office
NAS .... National Airspace System
NIRS .... Noise Impact Routing System
NO_X .... Oxides of Nitrogen
OEP .... Operational Evolutionary Plan
OPR .... Overall Pressure Ratio
PARTNER .... Partnership for Air Transportation Noise and Emission Reduction
PM .... Particulate Matter
SAGE .... System for assessing Aviation's Global Emissions
SDO .... Super Density Operations
SMAD .... Systems Modeling & Analysis Division
SO_X .... Oxides of Sulfur
VOC .... Volatile Organic Compounds

Acknowledgements

We thank Nick Miller of the JPDO EWG Science/Metrics Standing Committee for his assistance with the noise effects section of this report.

7 Appendix A: Super Density Operations environmental analysis

This analysis looks at the potential impacts of Super Density Operations (SDO) on an example airport, in this case Kennedy International Airport (JFK) near New York city. The results are not meant to be definitive, but rather to show the expected range of impacts.

7.1 Operations

Baseline operations at JFK for this analysis were taken from an ICAO study which looked at noise impact at the world's busiest airports. For this analysis, the individual aircraft types were consolidated down to five seat class representative aircraft. For the new aircraft analysis, the existing aircraft in the 150 and 300-seat classes were replaced with aircraft deemed technological viable in the relatively near future by the JPDO Environmental Working Group's Technology Panel. The Next Generation Single Aisle (NGSA) aircraft could be available in 2015, while the 777X could be available after 2020. These new aircraft would not replace the existing fleets immediately, since the airframe manufacturers could not produce a replacement number of aircraft in less than a decade, even if the airlines had the capital required to do this. For this analysis, the 2X and 3X scenarios are assumed to take place at a time in the future when the complete transition to these new types have taken place.

Also, because an airport in the following Metroplex analysis (see Appendix B) did not contain any arrival operations, arrival operations were also dropped from this analysis. The inclusion of the arrival tracks would increase the noise impacts shown below, but we can reasonably expect the changes to be proportional to the departure-only results given here.

Table 10, Aircraft consolidation

Seat Class	Existing Aircraft (engine type) used in analyses	New Aircraft
70	Embraer 145 (AE3007)	No change
150	Boeing 737-700 (CFM56-7)	NGSA
210	Boeing 757 (RB211-535)	No change
300	Boeing 777 (GE-90)	777X
400	Boeing 747-400 (P&W 4056)	No change

General aviation aircraft, turboprops, and helicopters were not included in the analysis. The operations at JFK by seat class for 2X and 3X operational increases are given below in Table 11. For the case where we assume a fleet mix shift to larger aircraft, we increase move the passengers from the 70 seat aircraft to the 150 seat aircraft, and move the passengers from the 210 seat aircraft to the 300 seat aircraft. Both larger aircraft in these cases are the new generation (NGSA and 777X, respectively). The increases in operations are scaled on the seat count increase (70/150 = 0.4667 NGSA operations for every 70 seat aircraft replaced, 210/300 = .7 777X operations for every 210 seat aircraft replaced).

Table 11, Departures at JFK by seat class

Seat Class	Baseline operations		2X (200%) operations		3X (300%) operations	
	Day	Night	Day	Night	Day	Night
70	40.2	5.8	80.4	11.6	120.6	17.4
150	114.3	32.3	228.6	64.6	342.9	96.9
210	52.8	9.8	105.6	19.6	158.4	29.4
300	97.6	22.1	195.2	44.2	292.8	66.3
400	18.8	8.4	37.6	16.8	56.4	25.2
Total operations	323.7	78.4	647.4	156.8	971.1	235.2

Table 12, Departures at JFK by seat class, shift to larger aircraft

Seat Class	Baseline operations		2X (200%) passengers		3X (300%) passengers	
	Day	Night	Day	Night	Day	Night
70	40.2	5.8	0.0	0.0	0.0	0.0
150	114.3	32.3	266.1	70.0	399.2	105.0
210	52.8	9.8	0.0	0.0	0.0	0.0
300	97.6	22.1	269.1	57.9	403.7	86.8
400	18.8	8.4	37.6	16.8	56.4	25.2
Total operations	323.7	78.4	572.8	144.7	859.3	217.0

7.2 Procedures

For this analysis, the impacts of the increase in operations are given in terms of 65 DNL noise levels, which are generally close to the airport; closer than any departure procedure changes would have an effect. For this reason, standard departure procedures (unrestricted departures without any type of ATC hold-downs) were used in the modeling for all scenarios.

7.3 Tracks

The tracks generated during initial study development for the ICAO analysis were used. Departures were assigned to runway 31L to mimic the Metroplex operations discussed below.

7.4 Impacts

The impacts of SDO are given in term of area (in square miles) exposed to noise levels higher than 65 DNL. The federal government considers residential housing an incompatible land use at this noise level. Table 13 below shows the results of this analysis.

Table 13, Noise impacts of SDO operations at JFK, 65 DNL Area in sq. miles

Fleet	1X (baseline) operations	2X (200%) operations/passengers	3X (300%) operations/passengers
Existing	5.0	9.2	12.6
New technology	-	6.0	8.6
Fleet shift	-	5.3	7.8

8 Appendix B: Metroplex environmental analysis

This analysis looks at the potential impacts of Metroplex operations on a regional system, in this case Kennedy International Airport (JFK), La Guardia airport (LGA), and Newark Liberty International (EWR) airports near New York city. The results are not meant to be definitive, but rather to show the expected range of impacts.

8.1 Operations

Baseline operations for this analysis at the three airports were taken from an ICAO study which looked at noise impact at the world's busiest airports. For this analysis, the individual aircraft types were consolidated down to five seat class representative aircraft. For the new aircraft analysis, the existing aircraft in the 150 and 300-seat classes were replaced with aircraft deemed technological viable in the relatively near future by the JPDO Environmental Working Group's Technology Panel. The Next Generation Single Aisle (NGSA) aircraft could be available in 2015, while the 777X could be available after 2020. These new aircraft would not replace the existing fleets immediately, since the airframe manufacturers could not produce a replacement number of aircraft in less than a decade, even if the airlines had the capital to do this. For this analysis, the 2X and 3X scenarios are assumed to take place at a time in the future when the complete transition to these new types have taken place.

Table 14, Aircraft consolidation

Seat Class	Existing Aircraft (engine type)	New Aircraft
70	Embraer 145 (AE3007)	No change
150	Boeing 737-700 (CFM56-7)	NGSA
210	Boeing 757 (RB211-535)	No change
300	Boeing 777 (GE-90)	777X
400	Boeing 747-400 (P&W 4056)	No change

General aviation aircraft, turboprops, and helicopters were not included in the analysis. The operations at JFK by seat class are given below in Table 15 (repeated from Appendix A for completeness), for LGA in Table 16, and EWR in Table 17.

Table 15, Departures at JFK by seat class

Seat Class	Baseline operations		2X (200%) operations		3X (300%) operations	
	Day	Night	Day	Night	Day	Night
70	40.2	5.8	80.4	11.6	120.6	17.4
150	114.3	32.3	228.6	64.6	3429	96.9
210	52.8	9.8	105.6	19.6	158.4	29.4
300	97.6	22.1	195.2	44.2	292.8	66.3
400	18.8	8.4	37.6	16.8	56.4	25.2
Total operations	323.7	78.4	647.4	156.8	971.1	235.2

Table 16, Departures at LGA by seat class

Seat Class	Baseline operations		2X (200%) operations		3X (300%) operations	
	Day	Night	Day	Night	Day	Night
70	118.7	7.9	237.4	15.8	356.1	23.7
150	186.2	28.8	372.4	57.6	558.6	86.4
210	32.0	6.1	64.0	12.2	96.0	18.3
300	0	0	0	0	0	0
400	0	0	0	0	0	0
Total operations	336.9	42.8	673.8	85.6	1010.7	128.4

Table 17, Departures at EWR by seat class

Seat Class	Baseline operations		2X (200%) operations		3X (300%) operations	
	Day	Night	Day	Night	Day	Night
70	365.8	30.4	731.6	60.8	1097.4	91.2
150	382.0	70.5	764.0	141.0	1146.0	211.5
210	114.9	19.9	229.8	39.8	344.7	59.7
300	59.9	13.6	119.8	27.2	179.7	40.8
400	4.5	2.9	9.0	5.8	13.5	8.7
Total operations	927.1	137.3	1854.2	274.6	9781.3	411.9

The original ICAO study for EWR did not contain any arrival operations. For this reason, only departures were considered in these Metroplex analyses. Also, the number of Newark departures in Table 17 above is almost certainly high; these numbers could realistically represent the total number of departures *and arrivals*. For this analysis we continued to use the departure numbers as given in the ICAO study.

8.2 Procedures

For this analysis, the impacts of the increase in operations are given in terms of 45 DNL noise levels, which are the lower limit for Air Traffic Management changes; at these relatively low noise levels, the change must be on the order of 5 dB for the FAA to consider the ATM changes as significant; this was discussed above in Table 1 of Section 2.1.

8.3 Tracks

The tracks generated during initial study development for the ICAO analysis were used. Figure 7 below shows all the tracks used at the different airports. Operations at all three airports were intended to model a North flow condition; only those tracks on runway 4L at EWR, runway 31L at JFK, and runway 31 at LGA were used. Figure 7 below shows the tracks used at the different airports. Note that thin blue tracks indicate departures, heavy red tracks indicate arrivals. Note that the scale indication in the figure is not accurate, since importing this graphic into document changed its physical size. Also note that Newark airport has no modeled arrival tracks.

In a full Metroplex study, we would model track changes which attempt to optimize the operation of the entire Metroplex. Such an analysis is beyond the scope of the current study.

Figure 7, Flight tracks from JFK, LGA, and EWR

8.4 Impacts

8.4.1 Noise

The impacts of regional Metroplex operations are given in term of area (in square miles) exposed to noise levels higher than 45 DNL. The federal government considers changes in exposure at this noise level due to air traffic changes to be potentially significant. Table 18 below shows the results of the Metroplex analysis.

Table 18, Noise impacts of Metroplex operations in the New York area, 45 DNL Area in sq. miles

Departure procedure	Fleet	1X (baseline) operations	2X (200%) operations	3X (300%) operations
Hold-down	Existing	**436.1**	601.2	695.5
	New technology	-	465.1	574.0
Un-restricted	Existing	**401.2**	538.2	**621.5**
	New technology	-	431.8	**527.6**

8.5 Graphical depiction of Impacts

The following figures show the impacts of increasing operations with the various fleets. The graphics are shown for the analyses in Table 18 above in **bold** font. Figure 8 and Figure 9 show the existing fleet with either all departures held down to eliminate traffic conflicts (Figure 8), or with all departures assumed to be un-restricted (Figure 9). For a depiction of the extreme case of operational increases, Figure 10 shows the 3X operations case with the existing fleet of aircraft, while Figure 11 shows the 3X case with the new technology NSGA and 777X aircraft. For these 3X cases, the assumption is un-restricted departures

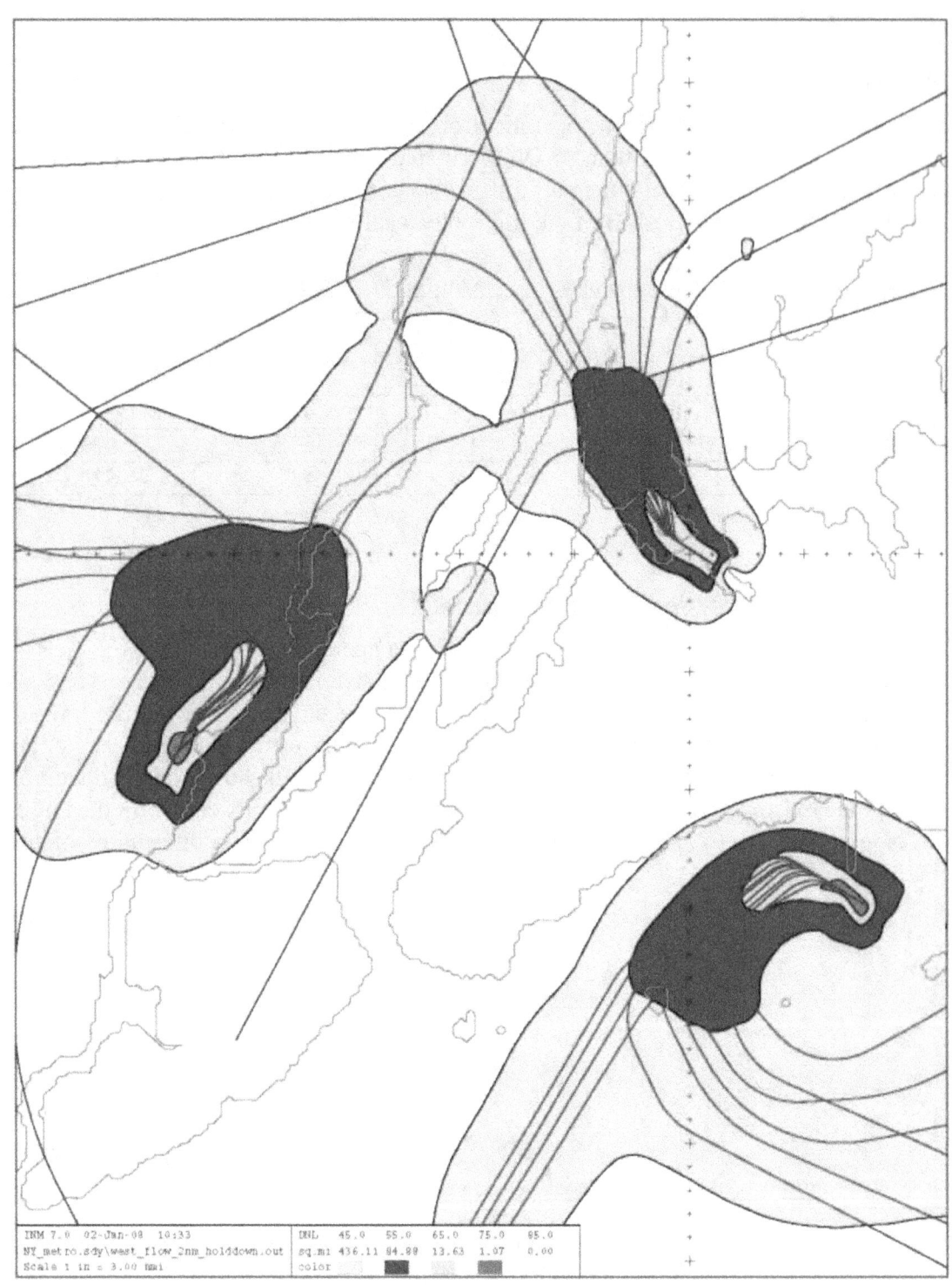

Figure 8, Noise impacts from existing departure, NYC Metroplex

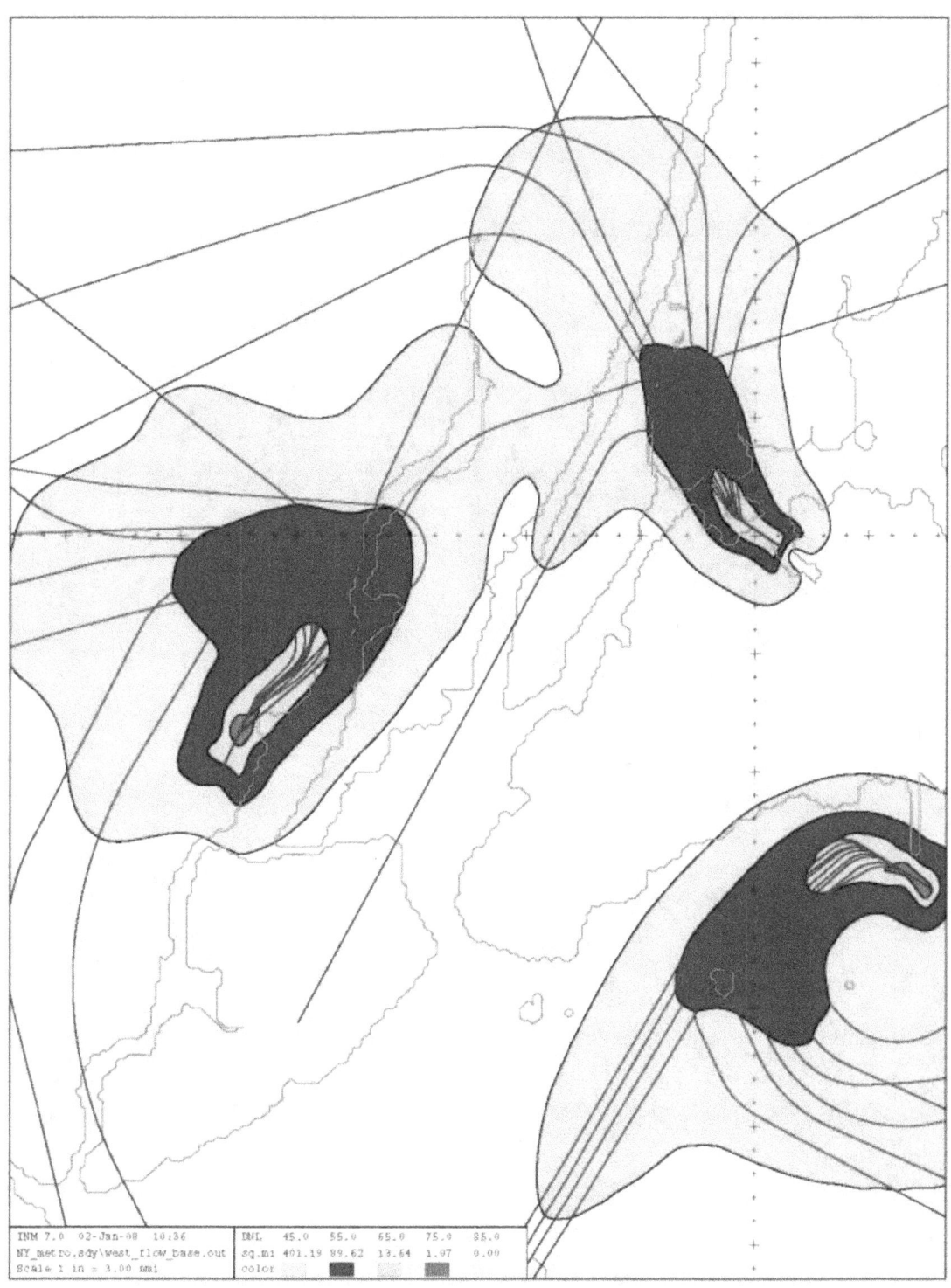

Figure 9, Noise impacts from unrestricted departures, NYC Metroplex

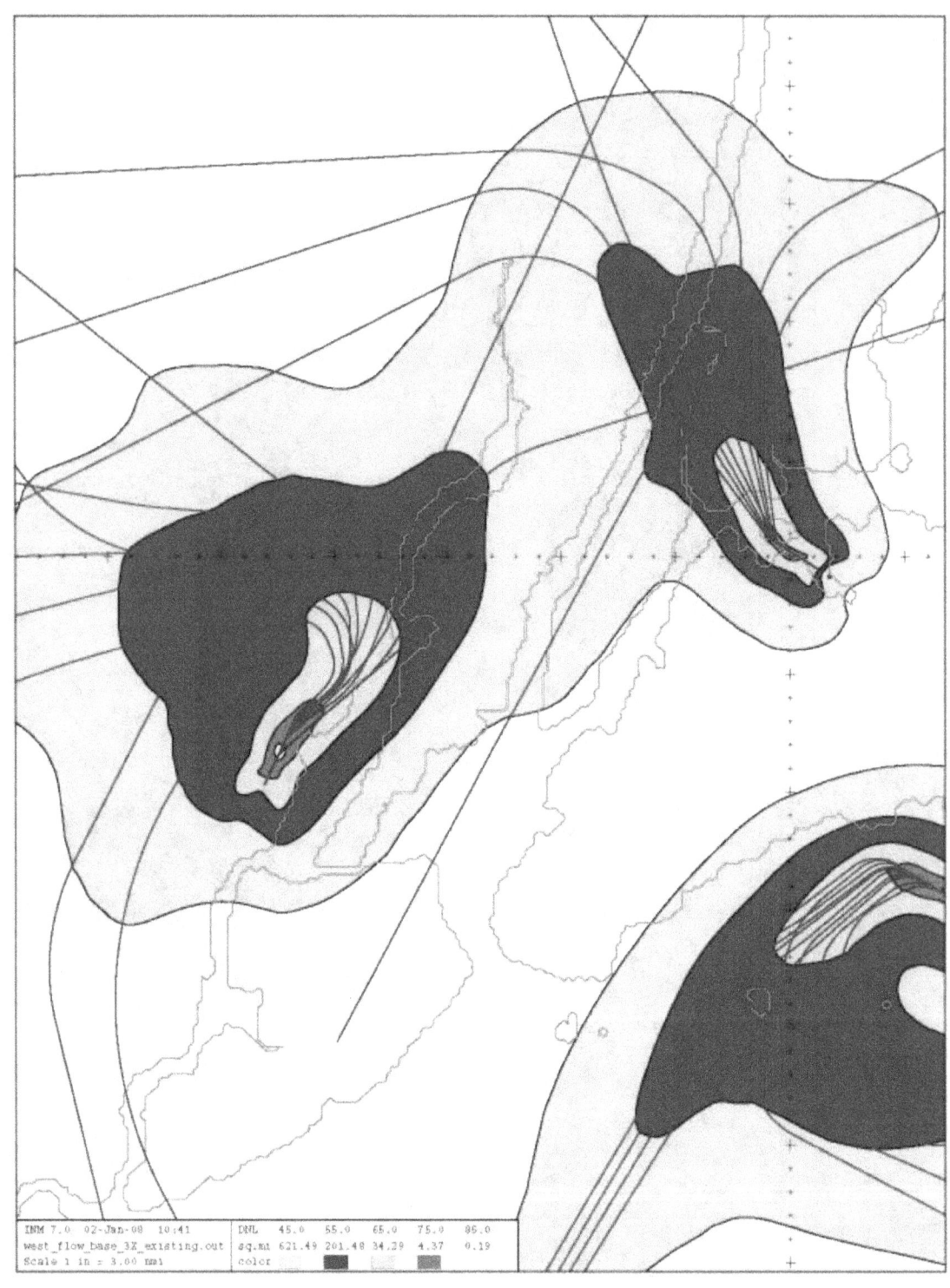

Figure 10, Noise impacts from 3X departure operations, existing fleet, NYC Metroplex

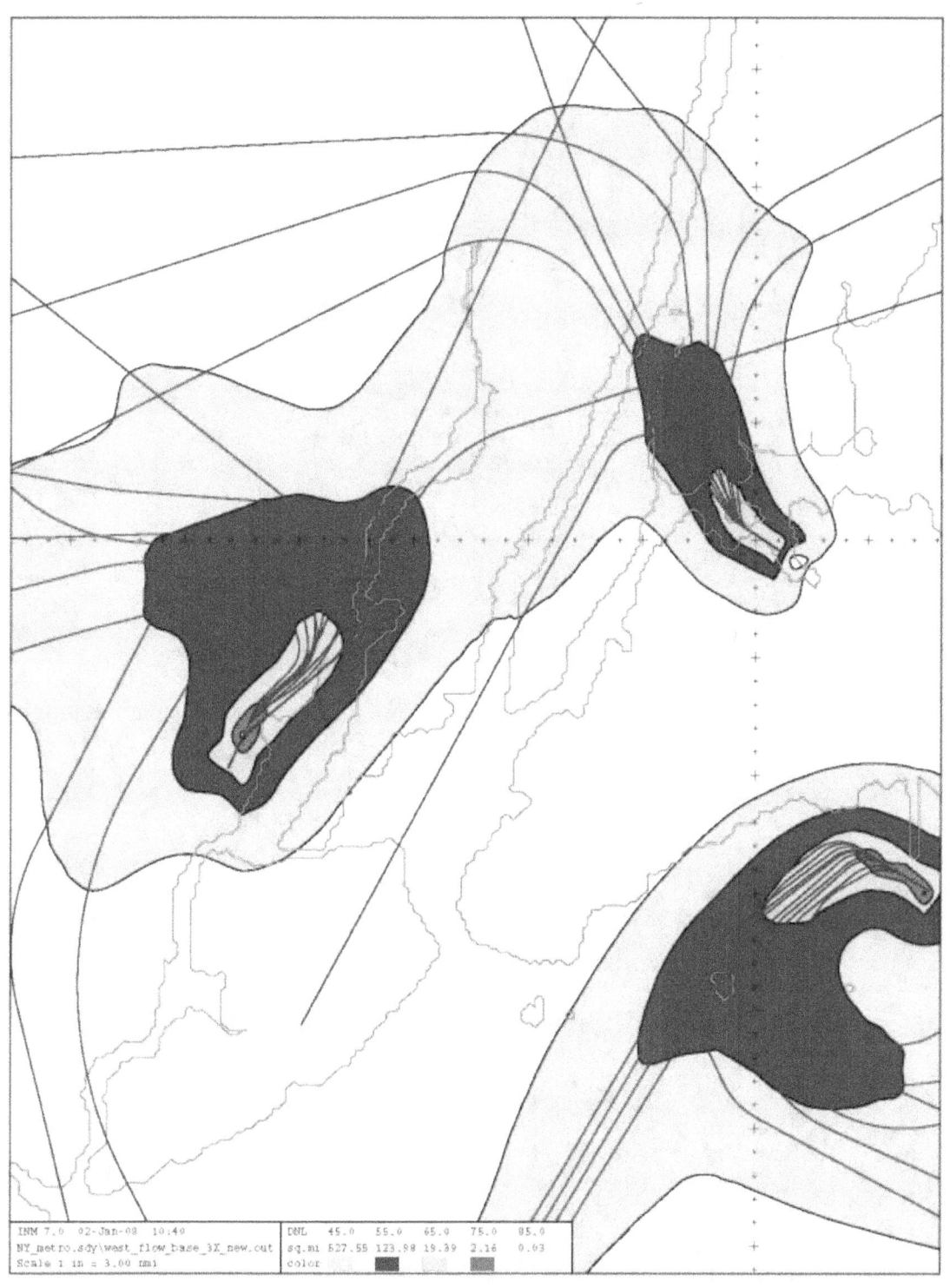

Figure 11, Noise impacts from 3X departure operations, new technology fleet, NYC Metroplex